low carb
recipes

DELICIOUS RECIPES FOR
ENJOYING A LOW-CARB DIET

LAUREN COLES

This is a Parragon Book
First published in 2004

Parragon
Queen Street House
4 Queen Street
Bath BA1 1HE

Created and produced by The Bridgewater Book Company Ltd.

ISBN: 1-40543-157-1

Printed in China

NOTE

*This book uses metric and imperial measurements. Follow the same units of
measurement throughout; do not mix metric and imperial. All spoon measurements
are level: teaspoons are assumed to be 5 ml and tablespoons are assumed to be 15 ml.
Unless otherwise stated, milk is assumed to be full fat, eggs and individual vegetables
such as potatoes are medium, and pepper is freshly ground black pepper.*

*Ovens should be preheated to the specified temperature. If using a fan-assisted oven,
check the manufacturer's instructions for adjusting the time and temperature.*

*Recipes using raw or very lightly cooked eggs should be avoided by infants, the elderly,
pregnant women, convalescents and anyone suffering from an illness. Pregnant and
breastfeeding women are advised to avoid eating peanuts and peanut products.*

Contents

Introduction

It is true that a balanced intake of all the food groups – fats, proteins and carbohydrates – in their appropriate proportions is the ideal that nutritionists encourage us to aim for. However, this begs a number of questions: where we are starting from, how old we are, what kind of lives we lead, whether we are men or women, and even how to estimate 'a balanced intake' and

'appropriate proportions'. Many of us have allowed the extra weight to creep on and developed bad eating patterns that make us sluggish, fat, unhappy and ill. A low-carbohydrate diet is one, very successful way of tackling these sorts of problems, revitalizing and re-energizing the system and trimming off that spare tyre.

What are Carbohydrates?

The name of this food group derives from the chemical elements it contains – carbon, hydrogen and oxygen – which form compounds such as starch and sugars. When these are eaten, the body breaks them down to release energy. They are found in a wide variety of commonly eaten foods. Grains and cereals, for example, feature in

most daily meals. Potatoes are a starchy staple and pulses, such as peas and beans, are also high in carbohydrates. Many popular snacks are packed with sugars. Carbohydrates are comfort foods, making us feel full and satisfied.

Dietary fibre is a second type of carbohydrate that our bodies can't digest. It helps to regulate the digestive system, but the body cannot break it down to release energy. This kind of carbohydrate is found in wheat bran, fruit, pulses, nuts and leafy green vegetables.

Energy and Body Weight

The body needs energy to function and it obtains this from the food consumed. Even the process of digestion uses up energy. However, the amount of energy you require depends on a number of factors. It is obvious that an Olympic athlete requires more input than a sedentary office worker, but age is also a consideration as the

metabolism begins to slow down from about the age of 30. Body type, including the amount of muscle mass and lean tissue, also affects energy requirements.

Energy is measured as calories, also called kilocalories (kcal) and as kilojoules (kJ). 1 kcal equals about 4 kJ. Many of the calories consumed are used quite quickly for everyday activities from breathing to walking up the stairs. The energy that is not used is converted by the body to be stored in the muscles or as fat. It is easy to see

that if you consume more calories than you use, the body will build up a store of fat.

The following is a guide to the approximate daily calorie intake required by men and women at different stages in life.

Growing children
Boys and girls – 1,800–2,220 calories per day

Adults who exercise/have physical jobs
Men – 2,850 calories per day
Women – 2,150 calories per day

Adults who don't exercise/have sedentary jobs
Men – 2,400 calories per day
Women – 2,000 calories per day

Over 50s
Men – 2,200 calories per day
Women – 1,850 calories per day

Low-carb Benefits

Carbohydrates are the main source of energy in our diets, with fats second, so if you want to lose weight, reducing their intake is a good way to do it. However, cutting them out all together is neither sensible nor practical, as you will also be cutting out important nutrients. It is also unwise to embark on a drastic reduction of carbohydrates all at once. If you introduce this new eating pattern gradually, you will not encounter the mood swings or hunger pangs that so often go with attempts to diet and usually result in failure.

While it is true that taking in more energy than is expended is the reason why fat accumulates in the body, the individual metabolism also plays a role. Some people are simply more intolerant of carbohydrates than others and can almost see their hips growing with every slice of crispbread. Pay close attention to your body and respond to its particular requirements.

Previously, the most difficult aspect of a low-carbohydrate diet was deciding what to eat, not what to leave out. This is because much of the variety and contrast in our 'normal' meals is derived from incorporating carbohydrates. Who wants a burger without a bun, steak without chips or meatballs without spaghetti? This problem is now solved because this book provides a wealth of recipes for delicious, low-carbohydrate dishes that are easy to cook and will satisfy the appetite. All the thinking, planning and calorie counting has been done for you. The recipes, based on meat, poultry, eggs, cheese and vegetables, offer both variety and enjoyment.

For many people, a low-carbohydrate diet is a lifetime choice, used to maintain their optimum body weight. Others find it a quick way to shed a few pounds before a summer holiday or after an over-indulgent Christmas. The choice is, of course, personal, but do bear in mind that if you return to higher carbohydrate meals, you are likely to regain weight.

Ingredients

Labels providing nutritional information on packaged foods are not always as clear and helpful as they might be. However, carbohydrate content is normally included and covers both starches and sugars. Dietary fibre, non-digestible carbohydrates, is usually listed separately. Not all products include a measure of fibre, either because there isn't any or because figures are not available. You may find it helpful to know that 1 gram of carbohydrate supplies about 3.75 calories or 16 kilojoules of energy.

There is no reason why you shouldn't substitute one ingredient for another in any of these recipes, provided that it does not increase the carbohydrate count. While Brie contains only traces of carbohydrate, Stilton may have 2 grams per 100 grams – a small difference, but it will up the count. Cauliflower contains almost twice as much carbohydrate as broccoli. Also, bear in mind that some most unexpected foods, including accompaniments and drinks, are high in carbohydrates. These will contribute to the overall count. It's no good cooking a low-carbohydrate curry and serving it with a high-carbohydrate chutney. At the same time, there is no point in being obsessive. English mustard may contain about 19 grams of carbohydrate per 100 ml, but when did you last eat more than half a teaspoon at one sitting? The desserts contain more carbohydrates than the other recipes in this book, but are low in comparison to most other desserts.

There are some specially manufactured low-carbohydrate products on the market. These are often quite expensive and their labels require close scrutiny. Jams and spreads produced without added sugar will contain some natural fruit sugars but are generally a good buy. Low-carbohydrate baked goods may be life-savers for some, but vary in quality, while sugar-free sweets and chocolates, originally produced for diabetes sufferers, have a good reputation.

N.B. The nutritional analysis given for the recipes in this book does not include optional ingredients or serving suggestions.

Soups, Starters & Side Dishes

Cream of Chicken Soup

Tarragon adds a delicate aniseed flavour to this tasty soup. If you can't find tarragon, use parsley for a fresh taste.

serves 4

55 g/2 oz unsalted butter
1 large onion, chopped
300 g/10½ oz cooked chicken,
finely shredded
600 ml/1 pint chicken stock
salt and pepper
1 tbsp chopped fresh tarragon
150 ml/5 fl oz double cream

Croûtons (optional)
4 thick slices day-old bread
4 tbsp olive oil
fresh tarragon leaves, to garnish

Method

❶ Melt the butter in a large, heavy-based saucepan, add the onion and fry for 3 minutes. Add the chicken to the saucepan with 300 ml/10 fl oz of the stock.

❷ Bring to the boil, then simmer for 20 minutes. Remove the saucepan from the heat and leave to cool, then transfer the soup to a food processor or blender and process until smooth.

❸ Add the remainder of the stock and season to taste. Add the chopped tarragon, pour the soup into a tureen or individual bowls and add a swirl of cream.

❹ If you are making Croûtons, cut the bread into even-sized cubes. Heat the oil in a frying pan. Add the bread cubes and fry until golden brown and crisp. Drain on kitchen paper and reserve until required.

❺ Garnish the soup with fresh tarragon and serve with the Croûtons.

Nutritional Information

Calories	420	Sugars	4g
Protein	24g	Fat	33g
Carbohydrate	6g	Saturates	20g

Chilli & Watercress Soup

This delicious soup is a wonderful blend of colours and flavours. It is very hot, so if you prefer a milder taste, omit the seeds from the chillies.

serves 4

1 tbsp sunflower oil

250 g/9 oz smoked tofu (drained weight), sliced

90 g/3 oz shiitake mushrooms, sliced

2 tbsp chopped fresh coriander

125 g/4½ oz watercress

1 fresh red chilli, deseeded and finely sliced, to garnish

Stock

1 tbsp tamarind pulp

2 dried red chillies, chopped

2 kaffir lime leaves, torn in half

2.5-cm/1-inch piece fresh root ginger, chopped

5-cm/2-inch piece galangal, chopped

1 stalk lemon grass, chopped

1 onion, quartered

1 litre/1¾ pints cold water

Method

❶ Put all the ingredients for the stock into a saucepan and bring to the boil.

❷ Simmer the stock for 5 minutes. Remove from the heat and strain, reserving the stock.

❸ Heat the sunflower oil in a preheated wok or large, heavy-based frying pan and cook the tofu over a high heat for about 2 minutes, stirring constantly so that the tofu cooks evenly on both sides. Add the strained stock to the frying pan.

❹ Add the mushrooms and coriander and boil for 3 minutes. Add the watercress and boil for a further 1 minute.

❺ Serve immediately, garnished with red chilli slices.

Nutritional Information

Calories 90

Protein 7g

Carbohydrate 2g

Sugars 1g

Fat 6g

Saturates 1g

Spinach & Ginger Soup

This mildly spiced, rich green soup is delicately scented with ginger and lemon grass. It makes a good light starter or summer lunch dish.

serves 4

2 tbsp sunflower oil

1 onion, chopped

2 garlic cloves, finely chopped

2 tsp finely chopped fresh root ginger

250 g/9 oz young spinach leaves

1 small lemon grass stalk, finely chopped

1 litre/1¾ pints vegetable stock

225 g/8 oz potatoes, chopped

1 tbsp rice wine or dry sherry

salt and pepper

1 tsp sesame oil

Method

❶ Heat the oil in a large saucepan. Add the onion, garlic and ginger and fry over a low heat, stirring occasionally, for 3–4 minutes until softened.

❷ Reserve 2–3 small spinach leaves. Add the remaining leaves and lemon grass to the saucepan, stirring until the spinach is wilted. Add the stock and potatoes to the pan and bring to the boil. Reduce the heat, cover the pan and simmer for about 10 minutes.

❸ Remove the pan from the heat and set aside to cool slightly. Tip the soup into a blender or food processor and process until completely smooth.

❹ Return the soup to the pan and add the rice wine or sherry, then adjust the seasoning to taste with salt and pepper. Heat until just about to boil.

❺ Finely shred the reserved spinach leaves and sprinkle some over the top. Drizzle a few drops of sesame oil into the soup. Ladle into warmed soup bowls, sprinkle the remaining shredded spinach on each and serve the soup immediately.

Nutritional Information

Calories	38	Sugars	0.8g
Protein	3.2g	Fat	1.8g
Carbohydrate	2.4g	Saturates	0.2g

Chinese Crab Soup

Two classic ingredients in Chinese cooking, ginger and soy sauce, are blended together in this recipe for a very special soup. Light soy sauce is used as it will not overpower all the other flavours.

serves 4

1 carrot, chopped	2.5-cm/1-inch piece fresh
1 leek, chopped	root ginger, grated
1 bay leaf	1 tsp light soy sauce
850 ml/1½ pints fish stock	½ tsp ground star anise
2 medium-sized cooked crabs	salt and pepper

Method

❶ Place the carrot, leek, bay leaf and stock into a large saucepan and bring to the boil over a medium heat. Reduce the heat, cover and leave to simmer for 10 minutes, or until the vegetables are nearly tender.

❷ Meanwhile, remove the meat from the cooked crabs. Break off the claws, break the joints and remove the meat (you may need a fork or skewer for this). Add the crabmeat to the stock in the saucepan.

❸ Add the ginger, soy sauce and star anise to the stock and bring to the boil. Reduce the heat and leave to simmer for 10 minutes, or until the vegetables are tender and the crab is heated through. Season to taste with salt and pepper.

❹ Ladle the soup into 4 warmed serving bowls and garnish with crab claws. Serve immediately.

Nutritional Information

Calories	145	Sugars	2.4g
Protein	40g	Fat	5.7g
Carbohydrate	2.7g	Saturates	2.6g

Griddled Smoked Salmon

It is best to buy packets of smoked salmon slices for this recipe as they lend themselves to folding more easily than freshly sliced salmon.

serves 4

350 g/12 oz sliced smoked salmon
1 tsp Dijon mustard
1 garlic clove, crushed
2 tsp chopped fresh dill
2 tsp sherry vinegar
4 tbsp olive oil

115 g/4 oz mixed salad leaves
salt and pepper

To garnish
fresh dill sprigs
mixed lemon, lime and orange slices

Method

❶ Fold the slices of smoked salmon, making 2 folds accordion-style, so that they form little parcels.

❷ To make the vinaigrette, whisk the mustard, garlic, dill, vinegar and seasoning together in a small bowl. Gradually whisk in the olive oil to form a light emulsion.

❸ Heat a ridged griddle pan over a medium heat until smoking. Add the salmon parcels and cook on one side only for 2–3 minutes until heated through and seared from the pan.

❹ Meanwhile, dress the salad leaves with some of the vinaigrette and divide between 4 serving plates. Top with the cooked smoked salmon, cooked side up. Drizzle with the remaining dressing. Serve, garnished with a few sprigs of fresh dill and a mixture of lemon, lime and orange slices.

Variation

This recipe would also work very well with smoked trout.

Nutritional Information

Calories	115	Sugars	1g
Protein	23g	Fat	15g
Carbohydrate	1g	Saturates	2g

Lettuce-wrapped Meat

Serve the minced meat and lettuce leaves on separate dishes:
each guest then wraps his or her own parcel.

serves 4

250 g/9 oz minced pork or chicken

1 tbsp finely chopped Chinese mushrooms

1 tbsp finely chopped water chestnuts

pinch of sugar

1 tsp light soy sauce

1 tsp Chinese rice wine or dry sherry

1 tsp cornflour

2–3 tbsp vegetable oil

½ tsp finely chopped fresh root ginger

1 tsp finely chopped spring onions

1 tbsp finely chopped Szechuan preserved
vegetables (optional)

1 tbsp oyster sauce

a few drops of sesame oil

salt and pepper

8 crisp lettuce leaves, to serve

Method

❶ Mix the minced pork with the Chinese mushrooms, water chestnuts, salt, pepper, sugar, soy sauce, rice wine and cornflour. Blend well until all the ingredients are thoroughly combined.

❷ Heat the vegetable oil in a preheated wok or large frying pan.

❸ Add the ginger and spring onions to the wok or frying pan, followed by the minced meat. Stir-fry for 1 minute.

❹ Add the preserved vegetables, if using, and continue to stir-fry for 1 minute.

❺ Add the oyster sauce and sesame oil, blend well and cook for a further 1 minute, or until the juices run clear. Transfer the mixture to a warmed serving dish.

❻ To serve, place about 2–3 tablespoons of the mixture on a lettuce leaf and roll it up tightly to form a small parcel. Eat with your fingers.

Nutritional Information

Calories	159	Sugars	0.2g
Protein	14g	Fat	10g
Carbohydrate	1g	Saturates	2g

Aubergine Satay

Aubergines and mushrooms are grilled on skewers and served with a satay sauce.

serves 4

2 aubergines, cut into 2.5-cm/1-inch pieces

175 g/6 oz small chestnut mushrooms

Marinade

1 tsp cumin seeds

1 tsp coriander seeds

2.5-cm/1-inch piece fresh
root ginger, grated

2 garlic cloves, lightly crushed

½ stalk lemon grass, roughly chopped

4 tbsp light soy sauce

8 tbsp sunflower oil

2 tbsp lemon juice

Peanut sauce

½ tsp cumin seeds

½ tsp coriander seeds

3 garlic cloves

1 small onion, puréed in a food processor
or chopped very finely by hand

1 tbsp lemon juice

1 tsp salt

½ fresh red chilli, deseeded and sliced

125 ml/4½ fl oz coconut milk

250 g/9 oz crunchy peanut butter

250 ml/8 fl oz water

Method

❶ Thread the vegetables on to 8 metal or presoaked wooden skewers.

❷ For the marinade, grind the cumin and coriander seeds, ginger, garlic and lemon grass. Stir-fry over a high heat until fragrant. Remove from the heat and add the remaining marinade ingredients. Place the skewers in a dish and spoon the marinade over. Leave to marinate for at least 2 hours and up to 8 hours.

❸ Preheat the grill. To make the sauce, grind the cumin and coriander seeds with the garlic. Add all the ingredients except the water. Transfer to a pan and stir in the water. Bring to the boil and cook until thick.

❹ Cook the skewers under the very hot grill for 15–20 minutes. Brush with the marinade frequently and turn once. Serve with the peanut sauce.

Nutritional Information

Calories	155	Sugars	2g
Protein	4g	Fat	14g
Carbohydrate	3g	Saturates	3g

Avocado Cream Terrine

The smooth, rich taste of ripe avocados combines well with thick, creamy yogurt and single cream to make this impressive terrine.

serves 4

2 ripe avocados
4 tbsp cold water
2 tsp gelazone (vegetarian gelatine)
1 tbsp lemon juice
4 tbsp low-fat mayonnaise
150 ml/5 fl oz natural yogurt
150 ml/5 fl oz single cream
salt and pepper
mixed salad leaves, to serve

To garnish
cucumber slices
nasturtium flowers

Method

❶ Peel the avocados and remove and discard the stones. Put the flesh in a blender or food processor or a large bowl with the water, vegetarian gelatine, lemon juice, mayonnaise, yogurt and cream. Season to taste with salt and pepper.

❷ Process for 10–15 seconds or beat by hand, using a fork or whisk, until smooth.

❸ Transfer the mixture to a small, heavy-based pan and heat very gently, stirring constantly, until just beginning to boil.

❹ Pour the mixture into a 900-ml/1½-pint terrine, non-stick loaf tin or plastic food storage box and smooth the surface. Allow the mixture to cool and set and then chill in the refrigerator for 1½–2 hours.

❺ Turn the terrine out of its container and cut into neat slices. Arrange a bed of salad leaves on 4 serving plates. Place a slice of avocado terrine on top and garnish with cucumber slices and nasturtium flowers.

Nutritional Information

Calories	327	Sugars	3g
Protein	6g	Fat	32g
Carbohydrate	4g	Saturates	8g

Thai Stuffed Omelette

This makes a substantial starter, or a light lunch or supper dish. Serve with a colourful, crisp salad to accompany the dish.

serves 4

2 garlic cloves, chopped

4 black peppercorns

4 fresh coriander sprigs

2 tbsp vegetable oil

200 g/7 oz minced pork

2 spring onions, chopped

1 large, firm tomato, chopped

6 large eggs

1 tbsp Thai fish sauce

¼ tsp ground turmeric

mixed salad leaves, tossed, to serve

Method

❶ Place the garlic, peppercorns and coriander in a mortar and, using a pestle, crush to a smooth paste.

❷ Heat 1 tablespoon of the oil in a large frying pan over a medium heat. Add the paste and fry for 1–2 minutes, until it just changes colour.

❸ Stir in the pork and stir-fry until it is lightly browned. Add the spring onions and tomato, and stir-fry for 1 minute, then remove the frying pan from the heat.

❹ Heat the remaining oil in a small, heavy-based frying pan. Beat the eggs with the fish sauce and turmeric, then pour one-quarter of the egg mixture into the frying pan. As the mixture begins to set, stir lightly to ensure that all the liquid egg is set.

❺ Spoon one-quarter of the pork mixture down the centre of the omelette, then fold the sides inwards towards the centre, enclosing the filling. Make 3 more omelettes with the remaining egg and fill with the remaining pork mixture.

❻ Slide the omelettes on to serving plates and serve with salad leaves.

Nutritional Information

Calories	250	Sugars	1g
Protein	21g	Fat	18g
Carbohydrate	2g	Saturates	4g

Easy Cauliflower & Broccoli

Whole baby cauliflowers are used in this recipe. Try to find them if you can, but if not use large florets instead.

serves 4

2 baby cauliflowers

225 g/8 oz broccoli

salt and pepper

Sauce

8 tbsp olive oil

4 tbsp butter or margarine

2 tsp grated fresh root ginger

juice and rind of 2 lemons

5 tbsp chopped fresh coriander

5 tbsp grated Cheddar cheese

Method

❶ Preheat the grill. Cut the cauliflowers in half and the broccoli into large florets.

❷ Cook the cauliflower and broccoli in a saucepan of boiling salted water for 10 minutes. Drain well, transfer to a shallow ovenproof dish and keep warm until required.

❸ To make the sauce, place the oil and butter in a frying pan and heat gently until the butter melts.

❹ Add the ginger, lemon juice, lemon rind and chopped coriander, and simmer for 2–3 minutes, stirring occasionally.

❺ Season the sauce with salt and pepper to taste, then pour over the vegetables in the dish and sprinkle the cheese on top.

❻ Cook under the hot grill for 2–3 minutes, or until the cheese is bubbling and golden brown. Leave to cool for 1–2 minutes, then serve.

Nutritional Information

Calories	433	Sugars	2g
Protein	8g	Fat	44g
Carbohydrate	3g	Saturates	9g

Roasted Vegetables

Rosemary branches can be used as brushes for basting and as skewers. Soak the rosemary skewers overnight to prevent them from charring.

serves 6

1 small red cabbage

1 fennel bulb

1 orange pepper, cut into
4-cm/1½-inch dice

1 aubergine, halved and sliced into
1-cm/½-inch pieces

2 courgettes, thickly sliced diagonally

6 rosemary twigs, about 15-cm/6-inches
long, soaked in cold water

olive oil, for brushing

salt and pepper

Method

❶ Preheat the barbecue or grill. Put the red cabbage on its side on a chopping board and cut through the middle of its stem and heart. Divide each piece into 4, each time including a section of the stem in the slice to hold it together.

❷ Prepare the fennel in the same way as the red cabbage.

❸ Blanch the red cabbage and fennel in boiling water for 3 minutes, then drain well.

❹ With a wooden skewer, carefully pierce a hole through the middle of each piece of vegetable.

❺ Thread a piece of orange pepper, fennel, red cabbage, aubergine and courgette on to each rosemary twig, gently pushing the rosemary through the skewer holes.

❻ Brush liberally with olive oil and season with plenty of salt and pepper.

❼ Cook over the hot coals or under the hot grill for 8–10 minutes, turning occasionally. Serve immediately.

Nutritional Information

Calories	16	Sugars	3g
Protein	1g	Fat	0.3g
Carbohydrate	3g	Saturates	0g

Long Beans
with Tomatoes

**Indian meals often need some green vegetables to complement the spicy dishes
and to off-set the richly flavoured sauces.**

serves 6

500 g/1 lb 2 oz French beans, cut into
5-cm/2-inch lengths

2 tbsp ghee

2.5-cm/1-inch piece of fresh
root ginger, grated

1 garlic clove, crushed

1 tsp turmeric

½ tsp cayenne pepper

1 tsp ground coriander

4 tomatoes, peeled, deseeded and diced

150 ml/5 fl oz vegetable stock

Method

❶ Blanch the beans briefly in boiling water, drain, refresh under cold running water and drain again.

❷ Melt the ghee in a preheated wok or large frying pan over a medium heat. Add the grated ginger and crushed garlic, stir and add the turmeric, cayenne and ground coriander. Stir over a low heat for about 1 minute until fragrant.

❸ Add the diced tomatoes to the wok, tossing until they are thoroughly coated in the spice mix.

❹ Add the vegetable stock to the pan, bring to the boil and simmer over a medium–high heat, stirring occasionally, for about 10 minutes, or until the sauce has reduced and thickened.

❺ Add the beans, reduce the heat to medium and heat through, stirring constantly, for 5 minutes.

❻ Transfer to a warmed serving dish and serve immediately.

Nutritional Information

Calories	76	Sugars	3g
Protein	2g	Fat	6g
Carbohydrate	4g	Saturates	3g

Mixed Leaf Salad

Make this green leafy salad with as many varieties of salad leaves and edible flowers as you can find to give an unusual effect.

serves 4

½ head frisée
½ head oakleaf lettuce
few leaves of radicchio
1 head chicory
25 g/1 oz rocket leaves
few fresh basil or flat-leaved parsley sprigs
edible flowers, to garnish (optional)

French dressing
1 tbsp white wine vinegar
pinch of sugar
½ tsp Dijon mustard
3 tbsp extra virgin olive oil
salt and pepper

Method

❶ Tear the frisée, oakleaf lettuce and radicchio into pieces. Place the salad leaves in a large serving bowl or individual bowls if you prefer.

❷ Cut the chicory into diagonal slices and add to the bowl with the rocket leaves and basil.

❸ To make the dressing, beat the white wine vinegar, sugar and mustard together in a small bowl until the sugar has dissolved. Gradually beat in the olive oil until the dressing is creamy and

thoroughly mixed. Season to taste with salt and pepper.

❹ Pour the dressing over the salad and toss thoroughly. Sprinkle a mixture of edible flowers, if using, over the top, and serve.

Cook's tip

Violas, hardy geraniums, nasturtiums, chive flowers and pot marigolds add vibrant colours and a sweet flavour to this salad. Use it as a centrepiece at a dinner party, or to liven up a simple everyday meal.

Nutritional Information

Calories 51
Protein 0.1g
Carbohydrate 1g
Sugars 0.1g
Fat 6g
Saturates 1g

Lobster Salad

Lobsters are best prepared simply, to ensure that none of the rich, sweet flavour is lost amid a mass of other ingredients.

serves 4

2 raw lobster tails	**Lemon-dill mayonnaise**
salt and pepper	1 large lemon
	1 large egg yolk
To garnish	½ tsp Dijon mustard
radicchio leaves	150 ml/5 fl oz olive oil
lemon wedges	1 tbsp chopped fresh dill
fresh dill sprigs	

Method

❶ To make the lemon-dill mayonnaise, finely grate the rind from the lemon and squeeze the juice. Beat the egg yolk in a small bowl and beat in the mustard and 1 teaspoon of the lemon juice.

❷ Using a balloon whisk or electric mixer, beat in the olive oil, drop by drop, until a thick mayonnaise forms. Stir in half the lemon rind and 1 tablespoon of the juice.

❸ Season with salt and pepper, and add more lemon juice if desired. Stir in the dill and cover with clingfilm. Place in the refrigerator to chill until required.

❹ Bring a large saucepan of salted water to the boil. Add the lobster tails and continue to cook for 6 minutes, or until the flesh is opaque and the shells are red. Drain immediately and leave to cool completely.

❺ Remove the lobster flesh from the shells and cut into bite-sized pieces. Arrange the radicchio leaves on individual plates and top with the lobster flesh. Place a spoonful of the lemon-dill mayonnaise on the side. Garnish with lemon wedges and dill sprigs and serve.

Nutritional Information

Calories	487	Sugars	2g
Protein	24g	Fat	42g
Carbohydrate	2g	Saturates	6g

Green Sesame Salad

A very elegant and light salad which will complement rice and noodle dishes beautifully.

serves 4

125 g/4½ oz beansprouts

1½ tbsp chopped fresh coriander

3 tbsp fresh lime juice

½ tsp mild chilli powder

1 tsp sugar

½ tsp salt

3 celery sticks

1 large green pepper, deseeded

1 large Granny Smith apple

2 tbsp toasted sesame seeds, to garnish

Method

1 Rinse the beansprouts and drain thoroughly.

2 Pick over the beansprouts, removing any that seem a little brown or limp – it is essential that they are fresh and crunchy for this recipe.

3 To make the dressing, combine the coriander, lime juice, chilli powder, sugar and salt in a small bowl and mix thoroughly.

4 Using a sharp knife, cut the celery into 2.5-cm/1-inch pieces. Cut the pepper into small pieces and the Granny Smith apple into small chunks.

5 Place the chopped celery, pepper, apple and beansprouts into a large mixing bowl and stir gently to mix.

6 Just before serving, pour the dressing over the salad, tossing well to mix.

7 Garnish the green sesame salad with the toasted sesame seeds and serve with rice or noodle dishes.

Cook's tip

Keeping each ingredient as fresh and crunchy as possible will make all the difference to this elegant salad. To prevent the apples from going brown, soak the slices briefly in a little lemon juice and water as soon as you have cut them.

Nutritional Information

Calories 78

Protein 3g

Carbohydrate 3g

Sugars 8g

Fat 3g

Saturates 0.5g

Chicory Salad

The contrast of the pink grapefruit, creamy chicory and bright green lamb's lettuce makes this dish look simply stunning.

serves 4

1 pink grapefruit	**French dressing**
1 avocado	3 tbsp olive oil
55 g/2 oz lamb's lettuce	1 tbsp wine vinegar
2 heads chicory, sliced diagonally	1 small garlic clove, crushed
1 tbsp chopped fresh mint	½ tsp Dijon or Meaux mustard
	1 tsp clear honey
	salt and pepper

Method

❶ Peel the grapefruit with a serrated knife. Cut the grapefruit into segments by cutting between the membranes. Set aside.

❷ To make the French dressing, put the oil, vinegar, garlic, mustard and honey into a screw-top jar and shake vigorously. Season to taste with salt and pepper. Pour the dressing into a bowl.

❸ Halve and stone the avocado and cut it into thin slices. Peel off the skin, put the sliced flesh into the bowl of French dressing and toss gently to coat.

❹ Remove any stalks from the lamb's lettuce and put into a bowl with the grapefruit, chicory and chopped mint.

❺ Add the avocado slices and 2 tablespoons of the French dressing. Toss well and transfer to individual serving plates. Serve immediately.

Cook's tip

Lamb's lettuce is so called because the shape of its dark green leaves resembles a lamb's tongue. It is also known as corn salad and the French call it mâche. It is easy to grow in the garden and will withstand the frost.

Nutritional Information

Calories	137	Sugars	4g
Protein	1g	Fat	13g
Carbohydrate	4g	Saturates	2g

Main

Courses

Barbecued Chicken

You need to put in a bit of effort to prepare the chicken, but once marinated it's a tasty candidate for the barbecue.

serves 4

1.5 kg/3 lb 5 oz whole chicken	2 fresh rosemary sprigs
grated rind of 1 lemon	1 small fresh red chilli, finely chopped
4 tbsp lemon juice	150 ml/5 fl oz olive oil

Method

❶ Split the chicken down the breastbone and open it out. Trim off excess fat, and remove the parson's nose, wing and leg tips. Break the leg and wing joints to enable you to pound it flat. This ensures that it cooks evenly. Cover the split chicken with clingfilm and pound it as flat as possible with a rolling pin.

❷ Mix the lemon rind and juice, rosemary sprigs, chilli and olive oil together in a small bowl. Place the chicken in a large dish and pour over the marinade, turning the chicken to coat it evenly. Cover the dish and leave the chicken to marinate for at least 2 hours in the refrigerator.

❸ Preheat the barbecue, then cook the chicken over hot coals for 30 minutes, turning it regularly until the skin is golden and crisp. To test if it is cooked, pierce one of the chicken thighs with a skewer; the juices will run clear, not pink, when it is ready. Serve.

Nutritional Information

Calories	129	Sugars	0g
Protein	22g	Fat	5g
Carbohydrate	0g	Saturates	1g

Chicken Fried in Banana Leaves

Leaves such as banana are often used in Thai cooking as a natural wrapping for all kinds of ingredients.

serves 4-6

1 garlic clove, chopped

1 tsp finely chopped fresh root ginger

¼ tsp pepper

2 fresh coriander sprigs

1 tbsp Thai fish sauce

1 tbsp whisky

3 skinless, boneless chicken breasts

2–3 banana leaves, cut into 7.5-cm/3-inch squares

sunflower oil, for shallow-frying

chilli dipping sauce, to serve

Method

❶ Place the garlic, ginger, pepper, coriander, fish sauce and whisky in a mortar and, using a pestle, grind to a smooth paste.

❷ Cut the chicken into 2.5-cm/1-inch chunks and toss in the paste to coat evenly. Cover and leave to marinate in the refrigerator for 1 hour.

❸ Place a piece of chicken on a square of banana leaf and wrap it up like a parcel to enclose the chicken completely. Secure with wooden cocktail sticks or tie with a piece of string.

❹ Heat a 3-mm/⅛-inch depth of oil in a large, heavy-based frying pan until hot.

❺ Shallow-fry the chicken parcels for 8–10 minutes, turning them over occasionally, until golden brown and the chicken is thoroughly cooked. Serve with a chilli dipping sauce.

Nutritional Information

Calories	185	Sugars	0g
Protein	18g	Fat	12g
Carbohydrate	0.5g	Saturates	1g

Beef with Wild Mushrooms

Choose fairly thick steaks for this dish to make it easier to cut the pockets.

serves 4

4 fillet or sirloin steaks

2 tbsp butter

1–2 garlic cloves, crushed

150 g/5½ oz mixed wild mushrooms, sliced if large

2 tbsp chopped fresh parsley

To serve

salad leaves

cherry tomatoes, halved

Method

❶ Preheat the barbecue. Place the steaks on a chopping board and, using a sharp knife, cut a pocket in the side of each.

❷ To make the stuffing, heat the butter in a frying pan, add the garlic and cook gently for about 1 minute.

❸ Add the mushrooms to the pan and cook gently for 4–6 minutes until tender. Stir in the parsley.

❹ Divide the mushroom mixture into 4 and insert a portion into the pocket of each steak. Seal the pocket closed with a

cocktail stick. If preparing ahead, let the mixture cool before stuffing the steaks.

❺ Barbecue the steaks over hot coals, searing the meat over the hottest part of the barbecue for about 2 minutes on each side. Move the steaks to an area with slightly less intense heat (usually the sides) and barbecue for a further 4–10 minutes on each side, depending on how well done you like your steaks.

❻ Transfer the steaks to serving plates and remove the cocktail sticks. Serve with salad leaves and cherry tomatoes.

Nutritional Information

Calories 414

Protein. 49g

Carbohydrate 1g

Sugars 0g

Fat. 24g

Saturates. 13g

Lamb with Bay & Lemon

Lamb chops are more elegant when the bone is removed to make noisettes.

serves 4

4 lamb chops	150 ml/5 fl oz lamb or vegetable stock
1 tbsp sunflower oil	2 bay leaves
15 g/½ oz butter	pared rind of 1 lemon
150 ml/5 fl oz white wine	salt and pepper

Method

❶ Using a sharp knife, carefully remove the bone from each lamb chop, keeping the meat intact. Alternatively, ask the butcher to prepare the noisettes for you.

❷ Shape the meat into rounds and secure with a length of string.

❸ Heat the oil and butter together in a large frying pan until the mixture begins to froth.

❹ Add the lamb noisettes to the frying pan and cook for 2–3 minutes on each side, or until browned all over.

❺ Remove the frying pan from the heat, remove the meat, drain off all of the excess fat and discard. Place the noisettes back in the frying pan.

❻ Return the frying pan to the heat. Add the wine, stock, bay leaves and lemon rind and cook for 20–25 minutes, or until the lamb is tender. Season the lamb and sauce to taste with a little salt and pepper.

❼ Transfer to serving plates. Remove the string from each noisette and serve with the sauce.

Nutritional Information

Calories	268	Sugars	0.2g
Protein	24g	Fat	16g
Carbohydrate	0.2g	Saturates	7g

Turkey with Cheese Pockets

Wrapping strips of bacon around the turkey helps to enclose the cheese filling.

serves 4

4 turkey breast pieces, about
225 g/8 oz each
salt and pepper
4 portions full-fat cheese (such as
Bel Paese), 15 g/½ oz each
4 sage leaves or ½ tsp dried sage
8 rashers rindless streaky bacon
4 tbsp olive oil
2 tbsp lemon juice

To serve
garlic bread
salad leaves
cherry tomatoes

Method

❶ Preheat the barbecue. Carefully cut a pocket into the side of each turkey breast. Open out each breast a little and season inside with salt and pepper.

❷ Place a portion of cheese into each pocket. Tuck a sage leaf into each pocket, or sprinkle with a little dried sage.

❸ Stretch the bacon rashers out with the back of a knife. Wrap 2 pieces around each turkey breast, covering the pocket.

❹ Mix the oil and lemon juice together in a small bowl.

❺ Barbecue the turkey over medium-hot coals, 10 minutes on each side, basting frequently with the lemon mixture.

❻ Place the garlic bread at the side of the barbecue and toast lightly. Transfer the turkey to warmed serving plates. Serve with the toasted garlic bread, salad leaves and cherry tomatoes.

Nutritional Information

Calories	518	Sugars	0g
Protein	66g	Fat	28g
Carbohydrate	0g	Saturates	9g

Citrus Duckling Skewers

The tartness of citrus fruit goes well with the rich meat of duckling. Duckling makes a delightful change from chicken for the barbecue.

serves 12

3 skinless, boneless duckling breasts

1 small red onion, cut into wedges

1 small aubergine, cut into cubes

Marinade

grated rind and juice of 1 lemon

grated rind and juice of 1 lime

grated rind and juice of 1 orange

1 garlic clove, crushed

1 tsp dried oregano

2 tbsp olive oil

dash of Tabasco sauce

Method

❶ Cut the duckling into bite-sized pieces. Place in a non-metallic bowl with the prepared vegetables.

❷ To make the marinade, place the lemon, lime and orange rinds and juices, garlic, oregano, oil and Tabasco sauce in a screw-top jar and shake until well combined. Pour the marinade over the duckling and vegetables and toss to coat. Leave to marinate in the refrigerator for 30 minutes.

❸ Preheat the barbecue. Remove the duck and vegetables from the marinade and thread them on to presoaked wooden skewers, reserving the marinade.

❹ Barbecue the skewers on an oiled rack over medium–hot coals, turning and basting frequently with the reserved marinade, for 15–20 minutes or until the meat is cooked through. Alternatively, cook under a preheated grill. Serve immediately.

Nutritional Information

Calories 205

Protein 24g

Carbohydrate 5g

Sugars 5g

Fat. 10g

Saturates 2g

Pork & Sage Kebabs

The pork mince mixture is shaped into meatballs and threaded on to skewers.
It has a slightly sweet flavour that is popular with children.

serves 6

450 g/1 lb minced pork

25 g/1 oz fresh breadcrumbs

1 small onion, very finely chopped

1 tbsp chopped fresh sage

2 tbsp apple sauce

¼ tsp ground nutmeg

salt and pepper

Basting mixture

3 tbsp olive oil

1 tbsp lemon juice

To serve

6 small pitta breads

mixed salad leaves

6 tbsp thick, natural yogurt

Method

❶ Place the minced pork in a mixing bowl with the breadcrumbs, onion, sage, apple sauce and nutmeg. Season to taste. Mix until the ingredients are well combined.

❷ Using your hands, shape the mixture into small balls about the size of large marbles. Place on a plate, cover with clingfilm and chill for at least 30 minutes.

❸ Meanwhile, soak 12 small wooden skewers in cold water for at least 30 minutes. Thread the pork meatballs on to the skewers. Cover with clingfilm and set aside in the refrigerator.

❹ Preheat the barbecue. To make the basting mixture, combine the olive oil and lemon juice in a small bowl, whisking with a fork until the mixture is well blended.

❺ Barbecue the kebabs over hot coals for 8–10 minutes, turning and basting frequently with the lemon and oil mixture, until the meat is golden brown and cooked through.

❻ Line the pitta breads with the salad leaves and spoon over some of the yogurt. Serve with the kebabs.

Nutritional Information

Calories	96	Sugars	0g
Protein	8g	Fat	7g
Carbohydrate	2g	Saturates	2g

Oyster Sauce Lamb

This really is a speedy dish, lamb leg steaks being perfect for
the short cooking time.

serves 4

450 g/1 lb lamb leg steaks

1 tsp ground Szechuan peppercorns

1 tbsp groundnut oil

2 garlic cloves, crushed

8 spring onions, sliced

2 tbsp dark soy sauce

6 tbsp oyster sauce

175 g/6 oz Chinese leaves

prawn crackers, to serve (optional)

Method

❶ Using a sharp knife, remove any excess fat from the lamb. Slice the lamb thinly.

❷ Sprinkle the ground Szechuan peppercorns over the meat and toss together until well combined.

❸ Heat the groundnut oil in a preheated wok or large, heavy-based frying pan.

❹ Add the lamb to the wok or frying pan and stir-fry for about 5 minutes.

❺ Meanwhile, crush the garlic cloves using a pestle and mortar. Add the garlic and spring onions to the wok together with the dark soy sauce and stir-fry for 2 minutes.

❻ Add the oyster sauce and Chinese leaves and stir-fry for a further 2 minutes, or until the leaves have wilted and the juices are bubbling.

❼ Transfer the stir-fry to warmed serving bowls and serve hot with prawn crackers, if using.

Cook's tip

Oyster sauce is made from oysters which are cooked in brine and soy sauce. Sold in bottles, it will keep in the refrigerator for months.

Nutritional Information

Calories 243

Protein 26g

Carbohydrate 3g

Sugars 0.4g

Fat 14g

Saturates 5g

Barbecued Herrings with Lemon

Cooking these fish in foil parcels gives them a wonderfully moist texture. They make a perfect dinner party starter.

serves 4

4 herrings, gutted and scaled

4 bay leaves

salt

1 lemon, sliced

4 tbsp unsalted butter

2 tbsp chopped fresh parsley

½ tsp lemon pepper

fresh crusty bread, to serve

Method

❶ Preheat the barbecue. Season the prepared herrings inside and out with salt to taste.

❷ Place a bay leaf inside the cavity of each fish.

❸ Place 4 squares of foil on the work surface and divide the lemon slices evenly between them. Place a fish on top of the lemon slices on each of the foil squares.

❹ Beat the butter until softened, then mix in the parsley and lemon pepper. Dot the flavoured butter liberally over the fish.

❺ Wrap the fish tightly in the foil and barbecue over medium–hot coals for 15–20 minutes, or until the fish is cooked through – the flesh should be white in colour and firm to the touch (unwrap the foil to check, then rewrap).

❻ Transfer the wrapped fish parcels to warmed serving plates.

❼ Unwrap the foil parcels just before serving and serve the fish with fresh crusty bread to mop up the deliciously flavoured cooking juices.

Nutritional Information

Calories	355	Sugars	0g
Protein	19g	Fat	31g
Carbohydrate	0g	Saturates	13g

Marinated Fish

Marinating fish, for even a short time, adds a subtle flavour to the flesh and makes even simply grilled or fried fish delicious.

serves 4

4 whole trout or mackerel, rinsed and gutted

4 tbsp chopped fresh marjoram

2 tbsp extra virgin olive oil

finely grated rind and juice of 1 lime

2 garlic cloves, crushed

salt and pepper

lime wedges, to garnish

green salad leaves, to serve

Method

❶ Using a sharp knife, cut 4 or 5 diagonal slashes on each side of the fish. Place the fish in a shallow, non-metallic dish.

❷ To make the marinade, mix together the marjoram, olive oil, lime rind and juice, garlic and salt and pepper in a bowl.

❸ Pour the mixture over the fish. Leave to marinate in the refrigerator for about 30 minutes.

❹ Cook the fish under a preheated grill for 5–6 minutes on each side, brushing occasionally with the reserved marinade, until golden.

❺ Transfer the fish to serving plates. Pour over any remaining marinade before serving, garnished with lime wedges and salad leaves.

Cook's tip

If the lime is too hard to squeeze, microwave on high power for 30 seconds to release the juice. This dish is also excellent cooked on the barbecue.

Nutritional Information

Calories 361

Protein 26g

Carbohydrate 0g

Sugars 0g

Fat 29g

Saturates 5g

Gingered Monkfish

This dish is a real treat and is perfect for special occasions. Monkfish
has a tender flavour, which is ideal with asparagus, chilli and ginger.

serves 4

450 g/1 lb monkfish	100 g/3½ oz fine asparagus
1 tbsp grated fresh root ginger	3 spring onions, diagonally sliced
2 tbsp sweet chilli sauce	1 tsp sesame oil
1 tbsp corn oil	

Method

❶ Cut the monkfish into bite-sized pieces. Mix the ginger and chilli sauce together in a bowl until thoroughly blended. Using a pastry brush, brush the ginger and chilli sauce mixture over the monkfish pieces.

❷ Heat the corn oil in a preheated wok or large, heavy-based frying pan.

❸ Add the monkfish, asparagus and spring onions to the wok and stir-fry for 5 minutes, stirring gently so the fish pieces and asparagus do not break up.

❹ Remove the wok from the heat, drizzle the sesame oil over the stir-fry and toss well to combine.

❺ Transfer the monkfish to warmed serving plates and serve immediately.

Cook's tip

Monkfish is quite expensive, but it is well worth using as it has a wonderful flavour and texture. You could use cubes of chunky cod fillet instead.

Nutritional Information

Calories	133	Sugars	0g
Protein	21g	Fat	5g
Carbohydrate	1g	Saturates	1g

Thai Spiced Salmon

Marinated in delicate Thai spices and quickly pan-fried to perfection, these salmon fillets are ideal for a special dinner. Serve them fresh from the frying pan to enjoy them at their best.

serves 4

2.5-cm/1-inch piece fresh
root ginger, grated
1 tsp coriander seeds, crushed
¼ tsp chilli powder
1 tbsp lime juice
1 tsp sesame oil
4 salmon fillet pieces with skin,
about 150 g/5½ oz each
2 tbsp vegetable oil
fresh coriander leaves, to garnish

To serve
stir-fried vegetables
freshly cooked rice

Method

❶ Mix the ginger, crushed coriander, chilli powder, lime juice and sesame oil together in a bowl.

❷ Place the salmon on a wide, non-metallic plate or dish and spoon the mixture over the flesh side of the fillets, spreading it to coat each piece of salmon evenly.

❸ Cover the dish with clingfilm and leave to chill in the refrigerator for 30 minutes.

❹ Heat a wide, heavy-based frying pan or ridged griddle pan with the vegetable oil over a high heat. Place the salmon in the hot frying pan, skin-side down, and cook for 4–5 minutes, without turning, until the salmon is crusty underneath and the flesh flakes easily.

❺ Serve immediately, with stir-fried vegetables and freshly cooked rice, garnished with coriander leaves.

Nutritional Information

Calories	329	Sugars	0g
Protein	30g	Fat	23g
Carbohydrate	0g	Saturates	4g

Fragrant Tuna Steaks

Fresh tuna steaks are very meaty – they have a firm texture, yet the flesh is succulent. Tuna is rich in valuable omega 3 oils.

serves 4

4 tuna steaks, 175 g/6 oz each

½ tsp finely grated lime rind

1 garlic clove, crushed

2 tsp olive oil

1 tsp ground cumin

1 tsp ground coriander

pepper

1 tbsp lime juice

fresh coriander, to garnish

To serve

avocado relish (see Cook's Tip)

tomato wedges

lime wedges

Method

❶ Trim the skin from the tuna steaks, rinse and pat dry on absorbent kitchen paper.

❷ In a small bowl, combine the grated lime rind, garlic, olive oil, cumin, ground coriander and pepper to taste, to make a paste.

❸ Spread the paste thinly on both sides of the tuna. Heat a non-stick, ridged griddle pan until hot and press the tuna steaks into the pan to seal them. Reduce the heat and cook for 5 minutes. Turn the fish over and cook for a further 4–5 minutes until the fish is cooked

through. Drain on kitchen paper and transfer to a warmed serving plate.

❹ Sprinkle the lime juice and fresh coriander over the fish. Serve immediately with avocado relish, and tomato and lime wedges.

Cook's tip

For the avocado relish, peel, stone and chop a small ripe avocado. Mix in 1 tablespoon lime juice, 1 tablespoon chopped fresh coriander, 1 finely chopped small red onion and some chopped mango or tomato. Season to taste.

Nutritional Information

Calories 239

Protein 42g

Carbohydrate 0.5g

Sugars 0.1g

Fat 8g

Saturates 2g

Butterfly Prawns

These prawns look stunning when presented on the skewers, and they will certainly be an impressive prelude to the main meal.

serves 2-4

500 g/1 lb 2 oz or 16 raw tiger prawns, shelled, leaving tails intact

juice of 2 limes

1 tsp cardamom seeds

2 tsp cumin seeds, ground

2 tsp coriander seeds, ground

½ tsp ground cinnamon

1 tsp ground turmeric

1 garlic clove, crushed

1 tsp cayenne pepper

2 tbsp oil

cucumber slices, to garnish

Method

❶ Soak 8 wooden skewers in water for 20 minutes. Cut the prawns lengthways in half down to the tail and flatten out to form a symmetrical shape.

❷ Thread a prawn on to 2 wooden skewers, with the tail between them, so that, when laid flat, the skewers hold the prawn in shape. Thread another 3 prawns on to these 2 skewers in the same way. Repeat until you have 4 sets of 4 prawns each.

❸ Lay the skewered prawns in a non-porous, non-metallic dish, and sprinkle over the lime juice.

❹ Combine the spices and the oil, and coat the prawns well in the mixture. Cover the prawns and chill for 4 hours.

❺ Preheat the barbecue or grill. Cook over hot coals or in a grill pan lined with foil under the grill for 6 minutes, turning once.

❻ Serve immediately, garnished with cucumber and accompanied by yogurt or a sweet chutney – walnut chutney is ideal.

Nutritional Information

Calories 183	Sugars 0g
Protein. 28g	Fat. 8g
Carbohydrate 0g	Saturates 1g

Scallops with Mushrooms

Scallops have a rich but delicate flavour. When sautéed with mushrooms and bathed in brandy and cream, they make a really special meal.

serves 2

15 g/½ oz butter

225 g/8 oz shelled scallops

1 tbsp olive oil

50 g/1¾ oz oyster mushrooms, sliced

50 g/1¾ oz shiitake mushrooms, sliced

1 garlic clove, chopped

4 spring onions, white and green parts sliced

3 tbsp double cream

1 tbsp brandy

salt and pepper

fresh dill sprigs, to garnish

basmati rice, to serve

Method

❶ Heat the butter in a heavy-based frying pan and fry the scallops for about 1 minute, turning occasionally.

❷ Remove the scallops from the pan with a slotted spoon and keep warm.

❸ Add the oil to the pan and heat. Add the mushrooms, garlic and spring onions and cook for 2 minutes, stirring constantly.

❹ Return the scallops to the pan. Add the double cream and brandy, stirring well to mix.

❺ Season to taste with salt and pepper and heat to warm through. Garnish with fresh dill sprigs and serve with rice.

Nutritional Information

Calories	350	Sugars	1g
Protein	31g	Fat	28g
Carbohydrate	1g	Saturates	4g

Spinach Frittata

A frittata is another word for a large, thick omelette.
This is an Italian dish, which may be made with many flavourings. Spinach is used
as the main ingredient in this recipe for colour and flavour.

serves 4

450 g/1 lb fresh spinach leaves

2 tsp water

4 eggs, beaten

2 tbsp single cream

2 garlic cloves, crushed

50 g/1¾ oz canned sweetcorn, drained

1 celery stick, chopped

1 fresh red chilli, chopped

2 tomatoes, deseeded and diced

2 tbsp olive oil

2 tbsp butter

25 g/1 oz pecan nut halves

2 tbsp grated pecorino cheese

25 g/1 oz fontina cheese, cubed

pinch of paprika

Method

❶ Cook the spinach in the water in a covered saucepan for 5 minutes. Drain thoroughly and pat dry on kitchen paper.

❷ Beat the eggs in a bowl and stir in the spinach, cream, garlic, sweetcorn, celery, chilli and tomatoes. Mix well.

❸ Heat the oil and butter in a 20-cm/ 8-inch heavy-based frying pan.

❹ Spoon the egg mixture into the frying pan and sprinkle with the pecan nut halves, pecorino and fontina cheeses and paprika. Cook, without stirring, over a medium heat for 5–7 minutes, or until the underside of the frittata is brown.

❺ Place a large plate over the frying pan and invert to turn out the frittata. Slide it back into the frying pan and cook the other side for a further 2–3 minutes. Serve the frittata straight from the frying pan. Alternatively, transfer to a serving plate.

Nutritional Information

Calories	307	Sugars	4g
Protein	15g	Fat	25g
Carbohydrate	6g	Saturates	8g

Aubergine Rolls

Thin slices of aubergine are fried in olive oil and garlic, and then topped with pesto sauce and finely sliced mozzarella.

serves 4

2 aubergines, thinly sliced lengthways

5 tbsp olive oil

1 garlic clove, crushed

4 tbsp pesto

175 g/6 oz mozzarella, grated

fresh basil leaves, torn into pieces

salt and pepper

fresh basil leaves, to garnish

Method

❶ Preheat the oven to 180°C/350°F/ Gas Mark 4. Sprinkle the aubergine slices liberally with salt and leave for 10–15 minutes to extract the bitter juices. Turn the slices over and repeat. Rinse well with cold water and drain on kitchen paper.

❷ Heat the olive oil in a large frying pan and add the garlic and aubergine slices, a few at a time. Fry the aubergine lightly on both sides. Remove with a slotted spoon and drain them on kitchen paper.

❸ Spread a little pesto onto one side of each of the aubergine slices. Top with the grated mozzarella and sprinkle with the torn basil leaves. Season with a little salt and pepper to taste. Roll up the slices and secure them with wooden cocktail sticks.

❹ Arrange the aubergine rolls in a greased ovenproof baking dish. Bake in the preheated oven for 8–10 minutes.

❺ Transfer the aubergine rolls to a warmed serving plate. Scatter with fresh basil leaves and serve immediately.

Cook's tip

You could use sliced courgettes instead of the aubergine. They will take less time to fry.

Nutritional Information

Calories	278	Sugars	2g
Protein	4g	Fat	28g
Carbohydrate	2g	Saturates	7g

Ma-Po Tofu

Ma-Po was the wife of a Szechuan chef who created this popular dish in the middle of the 19th century.

serves 4

3 packets firm tofu, about 8 oz/225 g each

3 tbsp vegetable oil

125 g/4½ oz coarsely minced beef

½ tsp finely chopped garlic

1 leek, cut into short sections

½ tsp salt

1 tbsp black bean sauce

1 tbsp light soy sauce

1 tsp chilli bean sauce

3-4 tbsp chicken or vegetable stock

2 tsp cornflour

3 tsp cold water

few drops of sesame oil

black pepper

finely chopped spring onions, to garnish

Method

❶ Drain the tofu and cut into 1-cm/½-inch cubes, handling it carefully.

❷ Bring some water to the boil in a small saucepan or a wok, add the tofu and blanch for 2-3 minutes to harden. Remove and drain well.

❸ Heat the oil in a preheated wok. Add the minced beef and garlic and stir-fry for about 1 minute, or until the colour of the beef changes. Add the leek, salt and sauces and blend well.

❹ Add the stock followed by the tofu. Bring to the boil and braise gently for 2-3 minutes.

❺ Mix the cornflour with the water until it forms a smooth paste, then add to the wok and stir until the sauce has thickened. Sprinkle with sesame oil and black pepper, garnish with spring onions and serve hot.

Cook's tip

Tofu has been an important element in Chinese cooking for more than 1000 years. Tofu is highly nutritious, being rich in protein and low in fat.

Nutritional Information

Calories 235	Sugars 1g
Protein 16g	Fat 18g
Carbohydrate 3g	Saturates 4g

Desserts

Coconut Sweet

Quick and easy to make, this sweet is very similar to coconut ice. Pink food colouring may be added towards the end if desired.

serves 4-6

75 g/2¾ oz butter

200 g/7 oz desiccated coconut

175 ml/6 fl oz condensed milk

few drops pink food colouring (optional)

Method

❶ Place the butter in a heavy-based saucepan and melt over a low heat, stirring constantly.

❷ Add the desiccated coconut to the melted butter, stirring to mix.

❸ Stir in the condensed milk and the pink food colouring, if using, and mix for a further 7–10 minutes, stirring constantly.

❹ Remove the saucepan from the heat, set aside and leave the coconut mixture to cool slightly.

❺ Once cool enough to handle, shape the coconut mixture into long blocks and cut into equal-sized rectangles. Leave to set for about 1 hour, then serve.

Cook's tip

Coconut is used extensively in Indian cooking to add flavour and creaminess to various dishes. The best flavour comes from freshly grated coconut, although ready-prepared desiccated coconut, as used here, makes an excellent standby. Freshly grated coconut freezes well, so it is worth preparing when you have the time.

Nutritional Information

Calories	338	Sugars	5g
Protein	4g	Fat	34g
Carbohydrate	5g	Saturates	26g

Italian Chocolate Truffles

These are flavoured with almonds and chocolate, and are simplicity itself to make.
Served with coffee, they are the perfect end to a meal.

makes 24

175 g/6 oz plain dark chocolate

2 tbsp almond-flavoured liqueur or
orange-flavoured liqueur

40 g/1½ oz unsalted butter

50 g/1¾ oz icing sugar

50 g/1¾ oz ground almonds

50 g/1¾ oz grated milk chocolate

Method

❶ Melt the plain dark chocolate with the liqueur in a bowl set over a saucepan of hot water, stirring until well combined.

❷ Add the butter and stir until it has melted. Stir in the icing sugar and the ground almonds.

❸ Leave the mixture in a cool place until firm enough to roll into 24 balls.

❹ Place the grated milk chocolate on a plate and roll the truffles in the chocolate to coat them.

❺ Place the truffles in paper sweet cases and leave to chill.

Variation

Almond-flavoured liqueur gives these truffles an authentic Italian flavour. The original almond liqueur, Amaretto di Saronno, comes from Saronno in Italy.

Nutritional Information

Calories	82	Sugars	7g
Protein	1g	Fat	5g
Carbohydrate	8g	Saturates	3g

Italian-style Strawberries

Generations of Italian cooks have known that the unlikely combination of freshly ground black pepper and ripe, juicy strawberries is fantastic.

serves 4-6

450 g/1 lb fresh strawberries

2–3 tbsp balsamic vinegar

pepper

fresh mint leaves, torn, plus extra to decorate (optional)

115–175 g/4–6 oz mascarpone cheese

Method

❶ Wipe the strawberries with a damp cloth, rather than rinsing them, so they do not become soggy. Using a paring knife, cut off the green stalks at the top and use the tip of the knife to remove the core or hull.

❷ Cut each hulled strawberry in half lengthways or into quarters if large. Transfer to a bowl.

❸ Add the balsamic vinegar, allowing ½ tablespoon per person. Add several twists of ground black pepper, then gently stir together. Cover with clingfilm and chill for up to 4 hours.

❹ Just before serving, stir in torn fresh mint leaves to taste. Spoon the mascarpone into bowls and spoon the strawberries on top. Decorate with a few mint leaves, if desired. Sprinkle with extra pepper to taste.

Cook's tip

This is most enjoyable when it is made with the best-quality balsamic vinegar, one that has aged slowly and has turned thick and syrupy. Unfortunately, the genuine mixture is always expensive. Less expensive versions are artificially sweetened and coloured with caramel.

Nutritional Information

Calories 132

Protein 1g

Carbohydrate 5g

Sugars 5g

Fat 12g

Saturates 7g

Mocha Swirl Mousse

A feather-light yet richly moreish combination, these chocolate and coffee mousses are attractively presented in tall glasses.

serves 4

1 tbsp coffee and chicory essence

2 tsp cocoa powder, plus extra for dusting

1 tsp low-fat drinking chocolate powder

150 ml/5 fl oz low-fat crème fraîche, plus 4 tsp to serve

2 tsp powdered gelozone

2 tbsp boiling water

2 large egg whites

2 tbsp caster sugar

4 chocolate coffee beans, to serve

Method

❶ Place the coffee and chicory essence in a bowl, and the cocoa powder and drinking chocolate in a second bowl. Divide the crème fraîche between the 2 bowls and mix both well.

❷ Dissolve the gelozone in the boiling water and set aside. In a grease-free bowl, whisk the egg whites and sugar until stiff and divide this evenly between the 2 mixtures.

❸ Divide the dissolved gelozone between the 2 mixtures and, using a large metal spoon, gently fold until well mixed.

❹ Spoon small amounts of the 2 mousses alternately into 4 serving glasses and swirl together gently. Place in the refrigerator and chill for about 1 hour, or until set.

❺ To serve, top each mousse with a teaspoonful of crème fraîche, a chocolate coffee bean and a light dusting of cocoa powder. Serve immediately.

Cook's tip

Gelozone, the vegetarian equivalent of gelatine, is available from most health food shops.

Nutritional Information

Calories 136

Protein 5g

Carbohydrate 11g

Sugars 10g

Fat 8g

Saturates 5g

Lemon Jumbles

These lemony, melt-in-the-mouth biscuits are made extra special by dredging with icing sugar just before serving.

makes 50

100 g/3½ oz butter, softened, plus extra for greasing

125 g/4½ oz caster sugar

grated rind of 1 lemon

1 egg, beaten

4 tbsp lemon juice

350 g/12 oz plain flour, plus extra for dusting

1 tsp baking powder

1 tbsp milk

icing sugar, for dredging

Method

❶ Preheat the oven to 160°C/325°F/ Gas Mark 3, then lightly grease several baking trays. Beat the butter, caster sugar and lemon rind together in a large bowl until pale and fluffy. Add the beaten egg and lemon juice, a little at a time, beating well after each addition.

❷ Sift the flour and baking powder into the creamed mixture and blend together. Add the milk, mixing to form a soft dough.

❸ Turn the dough out onto a lightly floured work surface and divide into 50 equal-sized pieces.

❹ Roll each piece into a sausage shape with your hands and twist in the middle to make an 'S' shape. Place the shapes on the baking trays and bake in the preheated oven for 15–20 minutes. Transfer to a wire rack and leave to cool completely. Dredge with icing sugar to serve.

Nutritional Information

Calories	50	Sugars	3g
Protein	1g	Fat	2g
Carbohydrate	8g	Saturates	1g

Exotic Fruit Parcels

Tempting pieces of exotic fruit are warmed through in a deliciously scented sauce
to make a fabulous barbecue dessert.

serves 4

1 pawpaw

1 mango

1 star fruit

1 tbsp grenadine

3 tbsp orange juice

single cream or low-fat natural yogurt,
to serve

Method

❶ Cut the pawpaw in half, scoop out the seeds and discard them. Peel the pawpaw and cut the flesh into thick slices.

❷ Prepare the mango by cutting it in half lengthways and carefully cutting the flesh away.

❸ Score each mango half in a criss-cross pattern. Push each half inside out to separate the cubes and cut them away from the peel.

❹ Using a sharp knife, thickly slice the star fruit.

❺ Place all of the fruit in a bowl and mix them together. Mix the grenadine and orange juice together and pour over the fruit. Leave to marinate for at least 30 minutes.

❻ Preheat the barbecue. Divide the fruit among 4 double thickness squares of foil and gather up the edges to form a parcel that encloses the fruit. Place the foil parcel on a rack set over warm coals and barbecue the fruit for 15–20 minutes.

❼ Serve the fruit in the parcel, with the low-fat natural yogurt.

Nutritional Information

Calories	43	Sugars	9g
Protein	2g	Fat	0.3g
Carbohydrate	9g	Saturates	0.1g

Rose Ice

This is a delicately perfumed sweet granita ice. It looks very pretty piled on a glass dish with rose petals sprinkled over.

serves 4

400 ml/14 fl oz water

2 tbsp coconut cream

4 tbsp sweetened condensed milk

2 tsp rosewater

few drops pink food colouring (optional)

pink rose petals, to decorate

Method

❶ Place the water in a small saucepan and add the coconut cream. Heat the mixture gently without boiling, stirring all the time.

❷ Remove from the heat and leave to cool. Stir in the condensed milk, rosewater and food colouring, if using.

❸ Pour the mixture into a large, freezerproof container and freeze for 1–1½ hours, or until slushy.

❹ Remove from the freezer and break up the ice crystals with a fork. Return to the freezer and freeze until firm.

❺ Spoon the ice roughly into a pile on a serving dish and sprinkle with rose petals to serve.

Cook's tip

To prevent the ice thawing too quickly at the table, nestle the base of the serving dish in another dish filled with crushed ice.

Nutritional Information

Calories	76	Sugars	9g
Protein	2g	Fat	4g
Carbohydrate	9g	Saturates	3g

Recipe List